聴覚障害者に対する図書館サービスのための IFLA 指針　第2版

ジョン・マイケル・デイ編

日本図書館協会障害者サービス委員会
　聴覚障害者に対する図書館サービスを考えるグループ訳

日本図書館協会

Guidelines for Library Service to Deaf People
2nd Edition
Edited by John Michael Day
(IFLA professional Reports, Nr.62)

© Copyright 2000 International Federation of Library Associations and Institutions

聴覚障害者に対する図書館サービスのためのIFLA指針 ／ ジョン・マイケル・デイ編 ； 日本図書館協会障害者サービス委員会聴覚障害者に対する図書館サービスを考えるグループ訳． － 第2版． － 東京 ： 日本図書館協会, 2003． － 66p ; 21cm． － Guidelines for Library Services to Deaf People, 2nd Editionの翻訳． －ISBN4-8204-0229-3

t1. チョウカク ショウガイシャ ニ タイスル トショカン サービス ノ タメノ イフラ シシン a1. ニホン トショカン キョウカイ s1. 聴覚障害 s2. 障害者と図書館 ①015.17

はじめに（初版）

　1990年代は聴覚障害者に対する図書館サービスの前進の上で、極めて重要な10年になるかもしれません。
　まず、1990年にはIFLA（国際図書館連盟）のストックホルム大会で、「聴覚障害者に対する図書館サービスのための指針」が採択されました。そして1991年には、世界ろう者会議が日本で開催されるにあたって、指針の編者であるジョン・マイケル・デイ氏が分科会で発表するために来日されることになりました。
　幸いにも、日本図書館協会では、障害者サービス委員会を中心に関係方面の協力を得て、障害者サービスを更に発展させるために、特に聴覚障害者サービスが日本に根付くことを願い、デイ氏に指針についての講演をしていただくことができました。
　ここに出版する小冊子『聴覚障害者に対する図書館サービスのためのIFLA指針－解説と講演会記録－』は、IFLAの指針の翻訳とデイ氏の講演会の記録をまとめたものです。翻訳には障害者サービス委員会の聴覚障害者に対する図書館サービスを考えるワーキンググループがあたりました。
　聴覚障害者の中でも特に障害が重度な方々の場合は、図書館と出会う機会さえ奪われていて、図書館を利用したことも利用したいと思ったこともないというのが実情でしょう。しかし、図書館員としては、こうした人たちの目を図書館に向けるためにどんな努力をしてきたかを省みる必要があります。わたくしたちが学ぶべきこと、身につけるべきことはたくさんあります。それでも、とにかく始めなければなりません。
　「国連・障害者の10年」は1992年で終わりましたが、「アジア太平洋

障害者の 10 年」が 1993 年から始まっています。図書館関係者だけでなく、障害者自身と障害者にかかわる多くの人々もお読みくださり、聴覚障害者に対する図書館サービスが進むことによって、聴覚障害者の情報環境が少しでも改善されることを願ってやみません。

1993 年 3 月

日本図書館協会障害者サービス委員会前委員長　西尾正二

第 2 版刊行にあたって

　本冊子は2000年に国際図書館連盟(IFLA)から出版された『Guidelines for Library Service to Deaf People』 2nd Edition を当グループで翻訳したものです。日本語訳初版は1993年に日本図書館協会から出版されました。

　改訂が必要になった経緯は「1. はじめに」に明らかですが、聴覚障害者への図書館サービスに、インターネット等の電子技術導入の必要性を説いた文献はまだ少ないので、貴重な資料となるでしょう。

　本文には、「この指針は各地の状況に合わせて容易に修正できるので、聴覚障害者に対する図書館サービスの全国的な指針を作る時の手引きとなるべきである」(p.20)とあります。日本ではこの日本語訳初版の7年前に、日本図書館協会から『聴覚障害者も使える図書館に－図書館員のためのマニュアル－』が刊行されています。1998年には、このマニュアルの改訂版が出ています。内容的にはIFLA指針にある「全国的な指針」とまでは言えませんが、本書と合わせて読んでいただければ、指針を日本でどう生かすべきかがわかると思います。

　日本語訳初版には、編者ジョン・マイケル・デイ氏が来日された際の講演「図書館の聴覚障害者サービスをどう進めるか－IFLA指針が目指すもの－」の記録と「大学図書館における聴覚障害学生に対するサービス」の講演要旨が収録されています。これらは指針初版に対応するものなので、今回は掲載を見送らざるを得ませんでした。

　ジョン・マイケル・デイ氏は、聴覚障害者のための教養系大学として世界唯一のギャロデット大学図書館長であり、1990年には、ワシントン大都市圏大学コンソーシアムの図書館評議会議長に選出されました。

アメリカ図書館協会では1989年から1990年まで「聴覚障害者に対する図書館サービスフォーラム」の議長でした。現在は、IFLAの「公共・学校図書館部会」の部会長と「不利な立場にある人々にサービスする図書館分科会」の議長を務めています。

日本語訳初版の冒頭に、「1990年代は聴覚障害者に対する図書館サービスの前進の上で、極めて重要な10年になるかもしれません」(p.3)とあります。しかし21世紀に入った今日、聞こえない人々にとって図書館がどれだけ役に立ち、身近なものになっているでしょうか。ある図書館でのコンピュータによる資料検索講習会に、聴覚障害者が自分で要約筆記者を連れて参加したという現実を知るにつけ、本冊子と『聴覚障害者も使える図書館に』改訂版の出版と普及が、聞こえない人々の情報環境の改善に役立つことを心から願っています。

2003年3月

日本図書館協会障害者サービス委員会聴覚障害者に対する
図書館サービスを考えるグループ

目　次

はじめに（初版） 3

第 2 版刊行にあたって 5

聴覚障害者に対する図書館サービスのための IFLA 指針 第 2 版 9

  1. はじめに 10

  2. 前文 18
    2.1　背景 18
    2.2　目的と範囲 20

  3. 指針 21
    3.1　職員 21
    3.2　コミュニケーション 25
    3.3　コレクション 30
    3.4　サービス 33
    3.5　プログラム・マーケティング（積極的広報活動） 36

  4. 定義 37

Guidelines for Library Service to Deaf People, 2nd Edition（原文）.... 41

あとがき 63

聴覚障害者に対する図書館サービスのためのIFLA指針　第2版

ジョン・マイケル・デイ編

　この指針は一般の図書館関係者のために書かれたものである。各国の図書館協会が、ここで想定されたものとは違う定義を持つ表現を一部修正したいと望む可能性があることは予期されるところである。この指針が示すように、「これは一般原則を述べており、範囲においては国際的なので、各国や各地方の実際上の制約条件によって調整されなければならない。」

編者

目次
1. はじめに 10
2. 前文 18
   2.1　背景 18
   2.2　目的と範囲 20
3. 指針 21
   3.1　職員 21
   3.2　コミュニケーション 25
   3.3　コレクション 30
   3.4　サービス 33
   3.5　プログラム・マーケティング（積極的広報活動） 36
4. 定義 37

1. はじめに

　国際的な指針への要求がはじめて生じたのは、1988年にオーストラリアのニューサウスウェールズ州立図書館が主催した聴覚障害者のための図書館サービスに関する会議中である。これに続く3年間は公式の指針作成にあてられ、最後に「国際図書館連盟」(IFLA)が承認して1991年に刊行された。過去10年の間に技術面で巨大な進歩があり、とりわけインターネットとワールドワイドウェブ(WWW)の発展は、例えばオンライン目録やデジタル情報データベースのように、図書館が情報を蓄積し提供する方法を根本から広げることになった。同様に聴覚障害コミュニティにおいても、構成員同士およびより大きな地域、国家、さらには国際的なレベルで個人や組織とコミュニケーションを行う方法に対して、こうした技術的進歩が大きな影響を及ぼした。例えば[南アフリカ共和国の]クワズールナタール州ろう協会(http://www.tradepage.co.za/kznda/)はWWWにウェブサイトを持っており、それほどまでにウェブが世界中で聴覚障害者に選ばれたことを表している。インターネットとWWWはコミュニケーション上の巨大な進歩であり、かつコミュニケーションは聴覚障害コミュニティに図書館サービスを提供する際のもっとも重要なところなので、指針初版の改訂が必要だった。加えるに、1991年の指針が実施されるようになってしかるべき批判が出てきており、「アメリカ図書館協会」(ALA)の部会の一つである「専門・協力図書館部会」(Association of Specialized and Cooperative Library Agencies〈ASCLA〉)がIFLA指針に修正を加える形でマーサ・L．ゴダード編『アメリカ聴覚障害コミュニティに対する図書館・情報サービスのための指針』(Guidelines for Library and Information Service for the American Deaf Community)を1996年に作成すると、この傾向はます

ます広範囲にわたるようになった。「専門・協力図書館部会」が自らの指針作成に際してIFLA指針から利点を引き出したように、この第2版も「専門・協力図書館部会」の指針にもとづいて作成された。

　第2版作成のための概要と理論的根拠は1998年のIFLAアムステルダム大会の「不利な立場にある人々にサービスする図書館分科会」(Libraries Serving Disadvantaged Persons〈LSDP〉)に提出され、同年秋には「世界ろう連盟」(World Federation of the Deaf〈WFD〉)にも配布された。最初の公式草案は1999年3月ウェールズのアバリストウィスにおける「不利な立場にある人々にサービスする図書館分科会」の常任委員会に提出された。そこで提案された修正を含めて、1999年8月オーストラリアで開かれた「世界ろう連盟」大会の期間に、検討と承認を求めるために「世界ろう連盟」に提出された。最終的な草案は同月、IFLAのタイ大会における「不利な立場にある人々にサービスする図書館分科会」の常任委員会で検討され受諾された。そしてIFLAの出版委員会に最終的な承認と出版を求めた。

　以下に掲げる人たちは、「不利な立場にある人々にサービスする図書館分科会」の常任委員会のメンバーであり、この第2版を作成するために、時間、努力、経験と専門的意見を惜しみなく与えてくれた。

Day, J.	（議長・アメリカ合衆国）
Tronbacke, B.	（書記／会計・スウェーデン）
Carlsen, K-J.	（ノルウェイ）
Craddock, P.	（イギリス）
Eltsova-Strelkova, V.	（ロシア連邦）
Galler, A.	（カナダ）
Guerin, C.	（フランス）

Irvall, B.	（スウェーデン）
Lithgow, S.	（イギリス）
Lehmann, V.	（アメリカ合衆国）
Mayol Fernandez, C.	（スペイン）
Skat Nielsen, G.	（デンマーク）
Pages Gilibets, T.	（スペイン）
Panella, N.	（アメリカ合衆国）
Stefanova, D.	（ブルガリア）
Strong, G.	（アメリカ合衆国）
Toran Marin, M.L.	（スペイン）
Diaz Roque, J.	（キューバ）

　マーサ・L．ゴダード氏にも特に感謝の意を表する。「専門・協力図書館部会」の『アメリカ聴覚障害コミュニティに対する図書館・情報サービスのための指針』の編者として、それを作成するためにIFLA指針初版を検討するにあたって、自らに課した大変な努力と、「専門・協力図書館部会」の「聴覚障害者に対する図書館サービスフォーラム」(Library Services to the Deaf Forum) での指導力とが、この第2版作成のための貴重な足掛かりを与えてくれた。

　聴覚障害者に図書館サービスを提供するための初版の指針作成は、IFLAの「不利な立場にある人々にサービスする図書館分科会」傘下の「聴覚障害者の要求を明らかにするワーキンググループ」(Working Group to Identify the Needs of the Deaf) の数年にわたる関心事であったし、それは当連盟の1988年の「中期活動プログラム」[注1]の一環と

[注1] International Federation of Library Associations [and Institutions]. Professional Board. *Medium Term Programme 1986 − 1991*. The Hague: IFLA Headquarters, 1988, pp.37 & 39.

して「公共・学校図書館部会」(Division of Library Serving the General Public)の指針準備プロジェクトに関連して行われたものである。この聴覚障害者サービスの指針作成プロジェクトは、編者とリーズ・ポリテクニク（イギリス）のウィリアム・アンダーソン氏、ワシントンDC公立図書館（アメリカ）のアリス・ハーゲマイヤー氏、ニューサウスウェールズ州立図書館（オーストラリア）のヴァレリー・ムーン氏との討論と手紙のやりとりの結果生まれたものである。まず、素案が、テキサス州ダラスで1989年6月に行われた「アメリカ図書館協会」の「聴覚障害者に対する図書館サービスフォーラム」の集会と、同年7月にワシントンDCで行われた「デフウェイ集会と式典」とで、検討と批評のために配布された。両集会での修正を経た最初の原案が、パリにおけるIFLAの1989年大会の期間に、ワーキンググループと分科会によって検討された。この最初の検討で変更された原案は、「世界ろう連盟」に審査のために送られ、ウィーンで行われた1990年1月の運営委員会(Management Committee)の会議中に検討された。［IFLAの］ワーキンググループと分科会常任委員会による検討も同年4月に行われた。この修正案は「世界ろう連盟」に評価のために送られ、1990年8月にブライトンで行われた理事会で同連盟の賛同を得た。そして、これが初版の最終案としてストックホルムにおけるIFLAの1990年大会で、「不利な立場にある人々にサービスする図書館分科会」に提出され、そこで正式に採択された。

　この指針を作成するにあたって、次に掲げる文献がこの主題の範囲を網羅することを保証し、首尾一貫した文体と型式の決定を助けるために検討された。特に『Library Service to the Deaf and Hearing Impaired』には感謝の意を表さなければならない。ダルトン氏のこの著作は、指針の準備において総合的な基準としての役割を果たしてくれた。

American Library Association. Association of Specialized and

Cooperative Library Agencies. "Techniques for Library Service to the Deaf and Hard of Hearing." *INTERFACE*, Fall, 1981.

American Library Association. Committee on Standards. *ALA Standards Manual.* Chicago, Illinois: American Library Association, January 1983.

Anderson, William. "Helping the Hard of Hearing". Unpublished manuscript. 1985.

Association of Specialized and Cooperative Library Agencies. Ad Hoc Subcommittee on Standards for Multitype Library Cooperatives and Networks. "Multitype Draft Standards". *INTERFACE*, Vol.11, (Fall, 1988)1, p.4.

Carroll, Frances Laverne, and Beilke, Patricia F. *Guidelines for the Planning and Organization of School Library Centres*, rev. ed., Paris: Unesco, 1979.

Cylke, Frank Kurt, ed. *Library Service for the Blind and Physically Handicapped: An International Approach*. München, etc.: K.G. Saur (IFLA Publications 16), 1979.

Dalton, Phyllis I. *Library Service to the Deaf and Hearing Impaired.* Phoenix, Arizona: The Oryx Press, 1985.

Hagemeyer, Alice. *Tentative Guidelines for Library and Information Services to the Deaf Community*. paper prepared for the American

Library Association. (Photocopy.), 1988.

International Federation of Library Associations [and Institutions]. Section of Libraries Serving Disadvantaged Persons. *Guidelines for Libraries Serving Hospital Patients and Disabled People in the Community.* The Hague: IFLA Headquarters, 1984 (IFLA Professional Reports, No.2).

International Federation of Library Associations [and Institutions]. Section of Public Libraries. *Guidelines for Public Libraries.* München, etc.: K.G. Saur (IFLA Publications 36), 1986.
邦訳：国際図書館連盟公共図書館分科会編　森耕一訳『公共図書館のガイドライン』（日本図書館協会　1987）

International Federation of Library Associations. Section of Public Libraries. *Standards for Public Libraries.* Pullach/München: Verlag Dokumentation, 1973.

Lynch, Beverly, ed. "Standards for University Libraries". *IFLA Journal*, Vol.13, (1987)2, pp.120-125.

Massis, Bruce E., ed. *Library Service for the Blind and Physically Handicapped: An International Approach.* Vol.2. München, etc.: K.G. Saur (IFLA Publications 23), 1982.

Moon, Valerie. *Opening Doors for Closed Ears: Proceedings of the Conference on Library Service for Deaf and Hearing Impaired People.* Sydney: State Library of New South Wales, 1988.

New York Library Association. Roundtable for Libraries Serving Special Populations. *Guidelines for Libraries Serving Persons with a Hearing Impairment or a Visual Impairment.* New York: New York Library Association, July 1987.

Sorenson, Liene S. *Taking Action to Enhance Public Library Services for Persons with Disabilities.* Skokie, Illinois: Skokie Accessible Library Services, Skokie Public Library, 1988.

　以下のリストに含まれるのは、「不利な立場にある人々にサービスする図書館分科会」の1990年の常任委員会メンバーやその他の人々であり、初版の指針を作成するために、時間、努力、経験と専門的意見を惜しみなく与えてくれた。

Anderson, W.	（イギリス）
Beaudin, J.	（アメリカ合衆国）
Bruhn, S.	（オーストラリア）
Carlsen, K-J.	（ノルウェイ）
Chavanis, G.	（フランス）
Coleman, J.	（アメリカ合衆国）
Czajkowski, F.	（ポーランド）
Dalton, P.I.	（アメリカ合衆国）
Dobbie, A.	（ニュージーランド）
Galler, A.	（カナダ）
Haimakainen, T.	（フィンランド）
Hagemeyer, A.	（アメリカ合衆国）
Kaiser, F.	（オランダ）
菊池　佑	（日本）

Law, C.　　　　　　　　　　（オーストラリア）
Malmgren-Neale, G.　　　　（スウェーデン）
Melkis, A.　　　　　　　　　（ドイツ連邦共和国）
Moon, V.　　　　　　　　　　（オーストラリア）
Noaks, P.　　　　　　　　　　（イギリス）
Peillon, M.　　　　　　　　　（フランス）
Pors, B.　　　　　　　　　　　（デンマーク）
Rappaport-Bathenau, G.　　（フランス）
Starmans, M.　　　　　　　　（オランダ）
Thulin, K.　　　　　　　　　　（スウェーデン）
Wagenaar, H.　　　　　　　　（オランダ）

　この指針の初版及び第2版の検討、提案、承認にあたり「世界ろう連盟」に対して深く謝意を表さなければならない。そしてIFLAと「世界ろう連盟」とは公式に協議する関係を確立したことを書きとめておく。

　　　　　　　　　　　　ジョン・マイケル・デイ
　　　　　　　　　　　　　ギャロデット大学図書館館長
　　　　　　　　　　　　　　アメリカ、ワシントンDC

　　　　　　　　　　　　不利な立場にある人々に
　　　　　　　　　　　　サービスする図書館分科会議長

2. 前文

2.1 背景

　多くの理由から、たいていの図書館は聴覚障害者に対する図書館サービスの提供について特に注意しようと考えてこなかった。聴覚障害者は一見しただけではそれとわからないし、聴者の社会にまじり合ってしまう傾向があるので、聴覚障害が「目に見えない障害」と呼ばれてきたのは無理もないことだ。その上、生まれた時から、あるいは幼い時から聞こえない人々は、多くの場合読むことが困難で、図書館を利用しようとしない。その結果、図書館と聴覚障害者はお互いのことをほとんど知らないできた。しかし、住民のかなりの部分が聴覚に障害があり、図書館側には、図書館の資料とサービスを聴覚障害者が利用できること、聴覚障害者に図書館が提供できるサービスは何かを聴覚障害者自身が知っていることを保証する責任がある。

　聴覚障害者に対するサービスの提供に関する主要な問題点は、コミュニケーションが多くの場合、普通以上の努力、知識、忍耐、それに科学技術的な補助機器（それが利用できるところでは）を必要とすることである。個々の聴覚障害者と言いたいことを伝え合うのにどの程度までこれらの特別な技能が必要かは、通常、その人の失聴程度と失聴年齢によって違ってくる。これらの個人差を理解するための核心は、失聴年齢による差異を理解することである。一般に、失聴年齢が高いほど音声・文字言語に対する気安さが大きいようだ。一方、生まれた時から聞こえないか、あるいは話すことを覚える前に聞こえなくなった人々は、理解しにくい話し方になるかもしれない。あるいは全く話さないかもしれな

いし、その上読むのが困難かもしれない。

　この相違のために、そして教育方法の相違のために、聴覚障害者はしばしばあれこれの名前をつけられて、分類されたり、分類しなおされたりしてきている。図書館員はこの相違と、教育やコミュニケーション方式に関する論争について知っている必要がある。それは聴覚障害に関する資料と、聴覚障害者と聴者のいずれもが関心と興味を持っているその他の関連資料からなる、幅広い、偏らないコレクションを作りあげるためである。聴覚障害者のためのプログラムを立案するにあたっては、この障害を持つ人々全部を包含する一つの用語があれば何かと便利である。そこで、この目的のために「聴覚障害コミュニティ」という言葉がこの指針で用いられるが、それは次のようなグループをまとめて指している。すなわち、手話常用者、手話と一般の人々が使う文字言語の両方を使う人、口話主義者、中途失聴者、老人性聴覚障害者、わずかな言語しか使わない人、難聴者、聴覚障害者家庭の聞こえる家族であり、聴覚障害コミュニティに対するサービスに携わる専門家も含まれる。「4. 定義」の「聴覚障害コミュニティ」を参照されたい。

　図書館は地域社会の偏らない情報の唯一の源というユニークな立場に立つことがよくある。そしてそれゆえに、聴覚に障害のある利用者にこのような情報を収集して提供する責任を負う。しかし、聴覚障害コミュニティに対するいかなる特別なプログラムでも、本来の目標は聞こえる利用者によって享受されているすべてのプログラムとサービスに対する平等なアクセスの提供であることを忘れてはならない。特別なプログラムとサービスの開始は、聴覚に障害がある利用者の特に加えられたニーズを認めた上での対応であるが、特別なプログラムが利用者の図書館経験のすべてになるべきではない。

2.2 目的と範囲

　この指針は、図書館員に聴覚障害者の図書館や情報についての要求を知らせるためのもので、利用者の一部に聴覚障害者がいるすべての図書館に適用される。政府、商業、工業、芸術、軍事、病院、矯正施設、その他の機関にサービスする専門図書館はもとより、公立図書館、学校図書館、学術図書館を含むあらゆるタイプの図書館に適用される。これは一般原則を述べており、そのために量的な規定を持たない。しかし、聴覚障害者のためのサービスを始めることに対する奨励としても、また、このようなサービスの完全さと質を評価する手段としても役立つことを意図している。この指針は範囲においては国際的なので、各国や各地方の実際上の制約条件によって調整される必要があること、たとえば科学技術や科学技術的な補助機器の使用に関する指針の適用は、そのようなものが利用できないところでは省かれるべきだということが理解されなければならない。

　さらに、この指針は各地の状況に合わせて容易に修正できるので、聴覚障害者に対する図書館サービスの全国的な指針を作る時の手引きとなるべきである。自分の国や地域に指針がない場合は、この指針を適用すべきである。

3. 指針

3.1 職員

3.1.1 聴覚障害コミュニティに対する図書館サービスの開発、実施、運営は、司書という専門的な地位にふさわしい学位や資格を持ち、訓練も受けたか、あるいはいずれか一つを持つか受けるかした専門職の図書館員が責任を持つべきである。

   解説

    図書館は利用者に可能な限り最良のサービスを提供しようと努力する。一般の利用者が利用できるのと同じ水準のサービスが、聴覚に障害のある利用者にも等しく利用できることは絶対必要である。この目標を達成するためには、訓練を受けた専門職の図書館員の注意が聴覚障害者向けサービスの計画と運営に必要である。そのサービスにどの程度まで継続的に専門職としての注意を集中すべきかは、図書館の規模、一般の地域社会の規模、聴覚障害コミュニティの規模といったことを含む多くの要素によって決まるだろう。しかしながら、専門職の図書館員がそのサービスに充てるべき時間は、それぞれの図書館の個々の事情による必要と実態に応じて十分であるべきである。聴覚障害コミュニティが非常に小さい図書館では、そのサービスの計画と管理は、その地区でもっと大きなサービスの責任を持つ専門職の図書館員によって最低限のことがなされるだけになるかもしれない。

3.1.2 図書館職員は、聴覚障害コミュニティに対するサービスの提供

にかかわる諸問題に焦点を絞った研修を受けるべきである。

解説

聴覚障害者に対して十分にして適切なサービスを提供するためには、職員が聴覚障害者の特別なニーズに対する理解を持つことが必要である。これらのニーズの中には、さまざまなコミュニケーション方法やろう文化、特別なコレクション、字幕付きのビデオ、補聴支援装置、特別な警報装置、科学技術を応用したコミュニケーション補助機器、読書力の水準、その他にかかわるものが含まれる(職員のコミュニケーション技術の研修に関する3.2.1をも見よ)。大都市地域では、職員の認識を深める研修を館内で行うために、聴覚障害者にサービスする他の地域グループの協力が得られるかもしれない。大都市地域以外では、職員の1人を正規の研修に派遣し、その職員に残りの職員を訓練する責任を持たせることしかできないかもしれない。

3.1.3 図書館は、聴覚障害者に対するサービスの提供に携わる職員を選ぶ時は、聴覚障害コミュニティで信頼されているか、あるいは信頼されることができそうな人を雇用しようと試みるべきである。

解説

他の少数派グループから雇用する場合も同じだが、図書館が聴覚に障害のある職員を雇うことには多くの利点がある。図書館は、聴覚障害コミュニティに対するサービスの責任者として、1人あるいはそれ以上の聴覚に障害のある専門職員または非専門職員を常勤か非常勤で雇うことができるかもしれない。聴覚障害者にサービスを提供するために職員を選ぶ時には、選ばれた人が必要な教育と経歴を持つこと、そして聴覚障害コミュニティで信頼されるだろうと期待させるような個性を示すことを、

またはそのどちらか一方を最低限図書館は保証すべきである。

3.1.4 図書館学部は、図書館員に専門的な資格を取る準備をさせるための基礎課程の正規の科目として、またすべての職階にいる図書館職員のための継続教育の科目として、聴覚障害コミュニティに対するサービス提供について訓練を行うべきである。

解説
現在、多くの図書館学部は、多様な住民にいかにサービスするかについて訓練を行っている。聴覚障害者に対するあらゆる種類のサービスの提供に関する訓練は、すべての専門職図書館員のための資格認定における必修科目であるべきだ。この訓練は、聴覚障害コミュニティに対する図書館サービス専門の独立した課程であるかもしれないが、それはこのような課程の設置を必要とするところに限られるだろう。訓練が、すべての不利な立場にある人々と多様な文化を持つ人々の両方、またはどちらか一方に対するサービスの提供に関するもっと幅広い課程に含まれる科目である場合も当然考えられる。

3.1.5 全国レベルの（適用できるところではしかるべき地域レベルの）責任を持つ図書館は、聴覚障害コミュニティに対する図書館サービスの提供について、その地理的範囲内にあるすべての図書館を援助するために、助言・相談サービスを提供する責任を持つ部局（office or department）を設けるべきである[注2]。

解説
一つの地理的範囲内でそのようなサービスを提供する責任を

注2.『公共図書館のガイドライン』（森耕一訳　日本図書館協会）p.62,「全国的な支援活動」6.9および6.10

持つ部局を設立することには、いくつかの利点がある。第一に、このような部局は、聴覚障害者にサービスを提供しているすべての図書館の間のネットワークの公式パイプとして機能するだろうし、それによって最新の技法、サービス、資料等が、[ネットワークに]参加する図書館の間で伝わることを保証するだろう。第二に、その地理的範囲内のすべての図書館における聴覚障害者に対するサービスの開始にあたって、誘因としての役割を果たすだろう。該当する地理的範囲の大きさとか、影響が及ぶ図書館の数とか、聴覚に障害のある住民全体の規模とかを含む多くの要素により、この部局はもっぱら聴覚障害者に対するサービスに責任を持つかもしれないし、あるいは他の不利な立場にある人々からなるグループに対するサービスも含む、もっと広い責任を持つかもしれない。

3.1.6 各国の図書館協会は、その組織内に聴覚障害コミュニティに対する図書館サービスの提供に専心する部門として機能するような会員グループを設けるべきである。

解説

聴覚障害者に対するサービスの提供にかかわる図書館員は、共通の関心を持つ諸問題を討議したり、全国レベルの協会に対して行動のための勧告を作成したり、情報を共有したりするための集会によって多くのことを得る。その上、そういう集会は、聴覚障害コミュニティに対する図書館サービスの提唱者として効果的に機能することができるだろう。

3.2 コミュニケーション

3.2.1 すべての図書館員は、聴覚障害者と確実に言いたいことを伝え合う方法の研修を受けるべきである。

解説

聴覚障害者はいろいろな方法で聴者と言いたいことを伝え合う。それぞれの生い立ちや聴力の程度、文化的背景、場面の違いに応じて手話を使ったり、話したり、書いたり、身振りをしたり、あるいはこれらを組み合わせて使うかもしれない。図書館サービスの提供に際して、図書館職員がこの多様性を認識することと、職員が不自由なく［聴覚障害者の言うことを］理解し、かつ［自分の言うことを］理解してもらうために何をなすべきかを知るのに必要な研修を受けることは必須である。聴覚に障害のある利用者が大勢いる図書館は、聴覚障害者に対するサービス提供に責任を持つ職員の少なくとも1人が、最低でも手話が中程度にうまいことと、他の利用者サービス担当職員がその任務にふさわしい程度に基本的な手話の経験を持つこととを保証するように、真剣に検討すべきである。

3.2.2 文字電話（TTY）は各図書館で、例えば参考業務カウンターのような、主要なサービスポイントで利用できるべきである。さらに、聞こえる利用者が図書館から電話することができるならば、聴覚障害者は少なくとも1台のTTYが利用できるようにするべきである(注3)。

注3. 科学技術における近年の進歩は、コミュニケーションに関するこの節に含まれる新しい補助装置、例えばTTY(3.2.2)、磁気ループ(3.2.6)等を利用可能にした。ただし、これらの装置は世界の多くの国々ではすぐには利用できないだろうし、そういうところでは

解説

　　TTYは聴覚障害者が電話するための手段である。聴者がレファレンス・サービスのために、あるいは図書館の開館時間等の一般的な情報を得るために図書館へ電話できるところでは、そして、公衆電話を図書館が備え付けているところでは、聴覚障害者が同じサービスを利用できるように、例えばTTYのような手段を提供すべきである。図書館職員は、全員がTTYの使用法の訓練を受けるべきである。

3.2.3　図書館の利用者や職員が使う電話は、音量増幅装置付き受話器を備えるべきである。

　　解説

　　例えば、音量調節器のような音量増幅装置付き受話器は、TTYを使わないで電話を使うに十分な残存聴力のある人を助ける。職員や利用者のための電話を備えている図書館では、音量増幅装置に頼って電話を使う人のためにこのような電話補助装置を備えるべきである。

3.2.4　図書館は、インターネットの自館のウェブサイトが完全に利用可能であることを保証すべきである。

　　解説

　　インターネットあるいはWWWにウェブサイトを持っている図書館では、提供された情報のすべてが聴覚に障害のある利用者にも利用可能であるようにする必要がある。音声はオープン

[装置のことは]無視すべきであるのは言うまでもない。この節における指針の真意は、聴覚に障害のある住民に対するサービスの提供においては、図書館は適切で利用可能な科学技術上の補助手段を何でも利用すべきであるということを示すことにある。

式字幕で表し、音声ファイルもダウンロード可能な文字ファイルとして利用できるようにすべきである。また、例えばウェブページを選ぶボタンを押した際のクリック音のように、音によるフィードバックが注意を促すために与えられる場合は、画面上のボタンが点滅するといった目に見えるフィードバックも与えられるべきである。

3.2.5 図書館は、聴覚障害コミュニティで有益だとわかった最新の技術を、聴覚障害者とのコミュニケーションのために利用すべきである。

解説

聴覚に障害のある利用者との即時のコミュニケーションのためにTTYを使用することに加えて、図書館は聴覚障害コミュニティで多数に受け入れられている技術は何であれ、容易で快適なコミュニケーションを保証するために利用すべきである。例えば、電子メールは聴覚障害者同士および聴覚障害者と聴者との間での非常に効果的なコミュニケーション方法であることがわかっている。したがって、インターネットが利用できるところでは電子メールによる図書館利用もできるようにすべきである。技術は変化するので、図書館は聴覚に障害のある利用者によって受け入れられ、広く使われているコミュニケーション方法に注意を払うべきである。というのは時がたてば、電子メールも、より新しくより効果的なコミュニケーション方法に乗り越えられることがあり得るからである。

3.2.6 図書館は、補聴支援システムや、パソコンによる同時字幕あるいはパソコン要約筆記に必要な器材設備のようなコミュニケーション補助機器を備えるべきである。これらの機器によるサービ

スは要求に応じて会合やプログラムのために利用できるようにすべきである。

解説

FM補聴システム、赤外線システム、磁気ループ等の補聴支援システムは、音声を大きくすることが必要な聴覚障害者によって使われる。これらの支援装置を使うことで、多くの利用者は講演、会合、音楽会、その他のプログラムをもっとよく理解することができる。パソコンによる同時字幕やパソコン要約筆記は、［手話等による］通訳者や補聴支援装置が役に立たない人にも、情報発生と同時に次々と文字になって出てくるのを読むことを可能にする。コミュニケーション技術は急速に変化しているので、図書館は最新の技術発展に常に注意を払い続けるべきである。

3.2.7　テレビの視聴設備がある図書館は、利用者が使うためのテレビのクローズド式字幕表示装置を備えるべきである。

解説

図書館は自分の国や地域の字幕挿入の基準に従って、クローズド式字幕付きであれ、あるいはオープン式字幕付きであれ、あるいは手話付きであれ、利用者のためにビデオテープを収集しておくべきである（3.3.4を見よ）。図書館がクローズド式字幕ビデオを収集しているところでは、ビデオテープを理解するために字幕に頼っている人が利用できるように、クローズド式字幕表示装置を備えるべきである。家庭での利用のためにクローズド式字幕付きビデオテープを貸出している図書館は、すべての聴覚障害者が利用者自身の技術製品の購買力にかかわりなく、同じ水準の情報とサービスの入手ができるように、貸出し用のクローズド式字幕表示装置をも備えるべきである。

3.2.8 図書館は、館主催のプログラムのすべてについて、要求があれば手話通訳、口話通訳、パソコン字幕、あるいはパソコン要約筆記を配置すると明示すべきである。

    解説

      書誌利用指導、コンピュータ講習、研究ワークショップ、ストーリーテリング等の一般市民向けの図書館関係のプログラムは、さまざまなコミュニケーション手段が必要な利用者が参加できるようにしなければならない。手話通訳、口話通訳、字幕表示の全部、またはそのうちの一つが、これらの手段に頼る利用者から出席の連絡があった時には、図書館の費用で提供されるべきである。

3.2.9 図書館は、非常事態や緊急事態を聴覚に障害のある利用者に知らせるために、視覚による警報信号装置を取り付けるべきである。

    解説

      聴覚障害者は火災報知機、拡声器、安全警報装置のような聴覚信号を聞きとれないので、図書館が聴覚に障害のある利用者に視覚によって館内放送を知らせ、緊急事態を警報するための装置を取り付けることは必須である。そのような装置は、聴覚信号が生じた時はいつでも閃光あるいは他の適切な目に見える信号を発するようにすべきである。図書館の館内点検あるいは避難訓練にあたっては、図書館職員と利用者の全員が、緊急事態について館内放送と通報の両方、またはどちらか一方を理解していることを保証すべきである。

3.3 コレクション

3.3.1 図書館は、聴覚障害者と聴者のいずれの利用者にも関心を持たれるような、聴覚障害とろう文化に関する資料を収集すべきである。

解説

聴覚障害者にサービスを提供するプログラムの本来の目的は、図書館のコレクション、プログラム、サービスのすべてを利用するに際して、聴覚障害者を一般の図書館利用者の中に組み入れることであろう。しかしながら、図書館は聴覚障害者にとって、また聴覚障害に関する情報を必要とするか、あるいは一般的な関心を持つ聴者にとって、特別な意味のある資料を収集することもすべきである。そのような資料は聴覚障害に関する最新資料と歴史的資料、聴覚に障害のある芸術家や他の有名な聴覚障害者による作品、および聴覚障害者に関する作品、手話その他のコミュニケーション方式に関する資料、政府刊行物、法律資料、聴覚障害に関する定期刊行物等を含むだろう。すべての領域の資源が聴覚に障害のある利用者に公開されるべきなので、これらの資料は物理的に切り離されたコレクションとして維持されるのではなく、図書館の資源全体に統合されるべきである。

3.3.2 図書館は、聴覚障害者のための教育上の選択肢や照会機関とプログラムに関する情報を、完全に公平な方法で収集し、維持し、提供すべきである。

解説

聴覚障害者の教育において採用された方法と聴覚障害者のコミュニケーション方式は、長年にわたって激しい論争と競争の

領域になっている。図書館は、公平で冷静な視点から十分な情報を提供するというユニークな立場に立つことがよくある。この立場ゆえに、図書館は、特に聴覚障害者、その親、他の家族、プログラムに携わる人々、照会機関のための情報のような領域において、資料をすべての観点から収集することを保証するように留意する責任を負う。

3.3.3 図書館は、聴覚障害者にとって興味がある、おもしろくて読みやすいレベルの資料のコレクションを収集し、利用できるようにすべきである(注4)。

解説

多くの聴覚障害者にとって、音声と文字による言語に熟達することは大変な困難である。図書館は、可能な限り多くの利用者に理解される一般的な資料を収集するよう努力すべきである。さらに、多くの聴覚障害者とその他の言語的少数グループ出身者を含む、その地方の音声・文字言語をまだ十分には獲得していない人々に容易に理解されるように、努めてわかりやすい簡単な語彙で書かれ、適切なところに豊富なさし絵が入った、おもしろい資料のコレクションを構築し、積極的に維持すべきである。

3.3.4 活字資料以外の視覚資料は、聴覚に障害のある利用者へのサービスを支えるために収集される図書館コレクションの必須の部分を形成すべきである。テレビ用の録画ビデオや音声を伴う他のこの種のメディアは、聴覚障害者に理解されるように字幕や手話が

注4. 国によっては、これらは"Easy-to-Read Materials"として知られている。[4.定義を見よ]

付けられるべきである。

解説

聴覚障害者は視覚に頼る必要があるので、視覚メディアはとりわけ情報伝達の有効な手段を提供する。そして、図書館の目標の一つが娯楽資料を提供することであるところでは、テレビ番組用のビデオテープは特に興味をそそる。オープン式字幕付きで製作されたビデオテープを収集するのが最も有効だろう。しかし、それが好ましくないところでは、図書館はクローズド式字幕付きビデオテープを収集すべきであり、必要なものとして字幕表示装置を提供すべきである（3.2.7を見よ）。

3.3.5 図書館は手話によるビデオテープと映画フィルム、あるいはいずれか一方のコレクションを収集・維持し、それを視聴するのに必要にして十分な設備を用意すべきである。

解説

手話は多くの聴覚障害者の生活において基本的なコミュニケーション手段である。手話によるビデオやフィルム、例えばテレビ番組の通訳、童話、デフ・フォークロア*、ニュース番組、手話指導等が製作されている国がある。可能なところでは、図書館はそのようなメディアを、聴覚障害者、聴覚障害児の親、手話を学んでいる人々に対する必須のサービスとして収集し、貸出すべきである。

*訳注：ろう者のジョーク、なぞなぞ、風刺漫画、伝説、経験談、手話研究、ゲーム、有名なろう者に関する物語等で、いずれも手話で伝えられてきたもの。

3.4　サービス

3.4.1　図書館のコレクション、サービス、プログラムはすべて、聴覚障害コミュニティがアクセスできるようにすべきである。

　解説

　　図書館が聴覚障害コミュニティを支えるために、自館のプログラムの一部分として始める特別なサービスに加えて、どうしても必要なのは、図書館にとってこれらのプログラムは聴者が利用できる自館のコレクション、サービス、プログラムをすべて聴覚障害者にも利用できるようにするという本来の目的の一部分にすぎず、この目的に付け加わるものであるという基本的な理解をもって、プログラムを設計し実行することである。例えば、情報検索のためのWWW利用講習のようなアクセス技術の講習会を図書館が提供している場合は、講習会に手話通訳を配置し、そのことを広報すべきである。

3.4.2　聴覚障害者に対する図書館サービスの企画と開発（それにはサービスの開発と資料の構築が含まれる）には、この指針で定義される聴覚障害コミュニティのメンバーが参加すべきであり、諮問委員会、サービス組織、ネットワークの設立についても同様である。

　解説

　　どんなサービスでも、その成功は内容と質、そして対象となる利用者がサービスを受け入れるかどうかにかかっている。サービスのプログラムが開始され、聴覚に障害のある図書館利用者内部で好評を得て成功したとわかる時期までは、プログラムの企画に責任ある担当者が地域社会へ出て行き、積極的に聴覚障害者の関与と援助を求めることが必要かもしれない。その

ような関係が設定された後は、サービスが引き続き成功するかどうかは、図書館と聴覚障害コミュニティとの間のこのネットワークが継続してうまくいくかどうかによるだろう。

3.4.3 図書館は手話を使ったプログラムを提供すべきである。
解説
　　図書館はその本質からいって、地域社会における主要な文化センターとなり、文化的・社会的プログラムを絶えず提供する。図書館で行われるすべてのプログラムと集会に、要求に基づいて手話通訳、口話通訳、パソコンによる同時字幕、パソコン要約筆記を付けて［聴覚障害者が］参加できるようにすることは必須である。それでもなお、ろう者のための手話によるプログラムも時には提供されるべきで、この場合は聴者のために手話を読んで音声に変える通訳者を配置する。手話によるプログラム、例えばストーリーテリングやろう文化に関するプログラムを提供することは、地域社会内のすべてのグループにとって興味深く、ためになるだろう(注5)。

3.4.4 図書館は、本を読めないろう者にも参加できる地域の識字プログラムに関する情報を提供すべきである。図書館は館主催の識字プログラムがろう者の要求を満たしていることを保証すべきである。
解説
　　生まれつき聞こえない、あるいは幼児期に聞こえなくなった人の多くは周囲で話される音声言語を聞きながら成長したのではないので、読むことを学ぶのが困難である。各国の手話はろ

注5. 『公共図書館のガイドライン』(森耕一訳　日本図書館協会) p.20 − 21 「文化活動」および p.2

う者の言語であり、音声言語とは全く異なる文法構造を持つ。図書館は識字プログラムを開発するにあたっては、最低限、ろう生徒の教育に使われた方法に精通している専門家と相談し、個々のろう者の独自の要求を考慮しなければならない。

3.4.5 図書館は自館の地域情報のオンライン・データベースに地域の聴覚障害に関する情報を含めるべきである。

解説

WWWの登場とともに、多くの図書館は、地域コミュニティ情報に中心となるレファレンスの核を提供するために、地域情報のオンライン・データベースを構築してきた。電子的コミュニケーションとWWWが聴覚障害者にとって極めて効果的なメディアであることがわかったので、図書館が聴覚に障害のある利用者にとって特に関心のある地域情報を提供するために、このような手段を使うことは重要である。

3.4.6 図書館は自館のオンライン・データベースに多種多様な聴覚障害に関するリンクを偏ることなく含めるべきである。

解説

世界的な聴覚障害団体とその関連団体は、聴覚障害者にとって関心のある情報を提供するのに、WWWを非常によく使っている。聴覚障害者により聴覚障害者のために提供されるレファレンス情報、文化情報、ニュース情報のたぐいまれな広がりと豊かさのゆえに、WWWが利用できる図書館では、このような情報が［聴覚障害者にも］利用できるようにする責任がある。ウェブページにそうしたリンクを張っている図書館は、収集したリンクが聴覚障害者やろう文化に関する多種多様な理念上の視点、文化的な視点を包含していることを保証するために、可

能なところでは、地域の聴覚障害コミュニティに幅広い支援を求めるべきである（指針 3.3.2 とその解説を見よ）。

3.5 プログラム・マーケティング（積極的広報活動）

3.5.1 図書館は、聴覚障害コミュニティに対して自館のプログラムとサービスを積極果敢に広報すべきである。

解説

　生まれた時から、あるいは幼い時から聞こえない人々はたいてい読むことが困難なので、一般に図書館を使おうとしない。そのため、聴覚に障害のある利用者を対象に特別な広報の努力をすることは、図書館にとって必須である。さもなければ、サービス提供に充てられた労働と資源はほとんど無駄になるだろう。同じ理由により、この努力は特に綿密な計画を必要とするだろう。

3.5.2 図書館の広報はすべて、聴覚障害コミュニティに届くような手段が講じられるべきである。

解説

　図書館は、聴覚障害者が利用できることを地域社会に知らせるために、あらゆる可能な手段を活用する必要がある。図書館はすべての便箋、お知らせ、パンフレット、ちらし等にTTY番号を入れるようにすべきであるし、テレビなどによる案内や広報にはすべて字幕を入れることを保証すべきである。図書館の一般向けの印刷物はすべて、聴覚障害者のためのプログラムとサービスに関する案内をも掲載すべきである。

4. 定義

　以下の用語はこの冊子中で使用されるもので、与えられた定義は図書館でこの指針を理解し、適用するのを助けることだけを目的とする。これらの用語をこの冊子の範囲外で適用することは意図していない。

Assistive Listening System（補聴支援システム）
　送信機と受信機からなる、聴力を補うシステム。一般的には、補聴器あるいは補聴器に接続された装置で、外部要因から生じる暗騒音*を取り除くように作られている。コミュニケーション補助システムにはいくつかの異なったタイプがあり、例えば磁気誘導ループシステム、AMシステム、FMサウンドシステム、赤外線システムがある。

　*訳注：対象としている音以外の音を総称して言う。バックグラウンド・ノイズ。

Audio Loop（磁気誘導ループ）
　Assistive Listening System（補聴支援システム）を見よ。

Captioned（字幕付き）
　映画フィルムやビデオで、画面に画像とともに会話も文字で表示されるものをいう。文字になった会話は、いつでも見える（オープン式字幕付き　open captioned）か、目に見えない信号を文字に変換する字幕表示装置を取り付けた場合だけ見える（クローズド式字幕付き closed captioned）かのどちらかである。

Closed Captioned
　　Captioned（字幕付き）を見よ。

Computer-Assisted Note Taking（パソコン要約筆記）
　　会合の間に話されていることを要約筆記者がパソコンのキーボードでタイプするシステム。その後わずかに遅れて、表示スクリーンかモニター画面に記録された文字が出てくる。

Computer-Assisted Real-Time Captioning（パソコンによる同時字幕）
　　非常に熟練した裁判所速記官が使う速記タイプと音声を文字に変換するパソコンによるシステム。ビデオモニターやスクリーンには、ただちに文字が一語一句そのままに出てくる。

Deaf Community（聴覚障害コミュニティ）
　　この用語はさまざまな文脈のもとでさまざまな意味を持つ。本書においては、以下の集団を指す。
・手話常用者
・手話と音声・文字言語の両方を使う人
・聴覚障害者で主に音声言語と読話によってコミュニケーションを行う人
・中途失聴者
・加齢により聞こえなくなった高齢者
・手話も文字言語も使わない聴覚障害者
・難聴者
・盲ろう者
・［聴覚障害者家庭の］聞こえる家族
・上記の人々に対するサービスに携わる専門家

Deaf Person（聴覚障害者）

部分的にか、あるいは全く聞こえない人。

Decoder（字幕表示装置）

テレビに外付けするか内蔵して、クローズド式字幕付きビデオの電気信号を、元のビデオ画像に沿って画面上で文字に変換する装置。

Easy-to-Read Materials（ER 資料）

おもしろくて読みやすいレベルの資料で、字幕付きメディアを含む。年齢にかかわりなく、読むことまたは理解することが困難なすべてのグループのためのもの。

Hard-of-Hearing Individual（難聴者）

中、軽度の聴力損失がある人。

Interpreters（通訳者）

音声コミュニケーションを手話かはっきりした口の動きかのいずれかに変換することに堪能な人。手話通訳者は音声言語の意味を手話に変えたり、手話を音声言語に変えることに堪能である。口話通訳者は、主として音声言語や読話でコミュニケーションを行う聴覚障害者に対して、話者の言葉を声を出さないで口の動きだけで通訳する。口話通訳者は手話を使わないで、読話しにくい言葉を［読話しやすい言葉に］置き換えることに堪能である。

Late-Deafened Adult（中途失聴者）

話すことを覚えた後で聞こえなくなった結果、生活の著しい変化を経験する成人。

Minimal Language User（わずかな言語しか使わない人）
　通常の音声言語、手話、あるいは文字言語について、非常に限られた知識しか持っていない人。

Native Sign Language User（手話常用者）
　第一言語が手話である人。

Open Captioned（オープン式字幕付き）
　Captioned（字幕付き）を見よ。

Oralist（口話主義者）
　聴覚障害者で主に音声言語と読話によってコミュニケーションを行う人。

TDD（聴覚障害者用遠距離通信装置）
　TTY を見よ。

TTY（文字電話）
　文字表示用ディスプレイとキーボードが付いた装置で、聞くことまたは話すことに障害がある人々に、視覚を通じた電話による双方向の通話を可能にする。

Visual Warning Signal（視覚による警報信号装置）
　火災警報または放送のような音声情報に聴覚障害者の注意をひくための閃光灯または回転灯。

Guidelines for Library Service to Deaf People

2nd Edition

聴覚障害者に対する図書館サービスのための IFLA 指針　第2版
原文

Edited by John Michael Day

International Federation of Library Associations and Institutions
IFLA Professional Reports, Nr. 62

©Copyright 2000 International Federation of Library Associations and Institutions

1. PREFACE

The need for international guidelines initially occurred during a conference on library services for deaf people hosted by the State Library of New South Wales, Australia in 1988 and the formal guidelines were developed over the next three years with final acceptance and publication by IFLA in 1991. Over these past 10 years, there have been enormous advances in technology, specifically the development of the Internet and the World Wide Web (WWW), which have fundamentally broadened the way libraries store and provide access to information, e.g., online catalogs and digital information databases. Likewise, these same technological advances have had a major impact on the way the deaf community communicates between and among its members and with individuals and organizations in the larger regional, national, and international communities, e.g., the electronic presence of the Kwa Zulu Natal Deaf Association on the WWW <http://www.tradepage.co.za/kznda/> is representative of the extend to which the web has been adopted by deaf people around the world. Because the Internet and the WWW are such major advances in communication and because communication is at the center of provision of library services to the deaf community, revision of the original guidelines was necessary. In addition, the 1991 guidelines have received the normal review that occurs as guidelines are put into practice; and, more extensively as the Association of Specialized and Cooperative Library Agencies (ASCLA), a division of the American Library Association, modified these IFLA guidelines in the development of their <u>Guidelines for Library and Information Services for the American Deaf Community</u>, 1996, ed. Martha L. Goddard. Just as ASCLA derived benefit from the original IFLA guidelines in the development of their own publication, so too has this 2nd edition built upon the work of ASCLA.

The outline and rationale for the development of the 2nd edition was presented to IFLA's Section of Libraries Serving Disadvantaged Persons (LSDP) during the 1998 IFLA Congress in Amsterdam and was shared with the World Federation of the Deaf (WFD) during the autumn of the same year. The first formal draft was subsequently presented to the LSDP Standing Committee during its meetings in Aberystwyth, Wales in March of 1999 and, incorporating changes as therein suggested, presented to the WFD for review and endorsement during their congress in, Australia, August, 1999. The final draft was reviewed and accepted by the LSDP Standing Committee later that same month during the IFLA Congress in, Thailand and released to IFLA's Publication Committee for final acceptance and publication.

The following persons are the members of the Standing Committee of the Section of Libraries Serving Disadvantaged Persons who have given freely of their time, effort, experience, and expertise in the development of this 2nd edition.

J. Day (Chair)	United States of America
B. Tronbacke (Secretary/Treasurer)	Sweden
K.-J. Carlsen	Norway
P. Craddock	United Kingdom
V. Eltsova-Strelkova	Russian Federation
A. Galler	Canada
C. Guerin	France
B. Irvall	Sweden
S. Lithgow	United Kingdom
V. Lehmann	United States of America
C. Mayol Fernandez	Spain
G. Skat Nielsen	Denmark
T. Pages Gilibets	Spain
N. Panella	United States of America
D. Stefanova	Bulgaria
G. Strong	United States of America
M. L. Toran Marin	Spain
J. Diaz Roque	Cuba

Special recognition is also due to Martha L. Goddard. As editor of the ASCLA Guidelines for Library and Information Services for the American Deaf Community, her own hard work and her leadership of the ASCLA Library Services to the Deaf Forum in the review of the 1st edition of these IFLA guidelines for the development of the ASCLA guidelines provided an invaluable stepping-stone in the development of this 2nd edition.

The development of original guidelines for the provision of library services to deaf people had been an interest of the Working Group to Identify the Needs of the Deaf within the IFLA Section of Libraries Serving Disadvantaged Persons for several years and was written in conjunction with the Division of Libraries Serving the General Public's project of preparation of guidelines as part of the 1988 Medium Term Programme of the Federation.[1] This project developed as a result of discussions and correspondence between the editor and Mr. William Anderson of Leeds Polytechnic, United Kingdom; Ms. Alice Hagemeyer of the District of Columbia Public Library, USA; and Ms. Valerie Moon of the State Library of New South Wales, Australia. The original outline from which subsequent drafts developed was distributed for review and comment at the meeting of the Library Services to the Deaf Forum of the American Library Association at its June, 1989 conference in Dallas, Texas and at the Deaf Way Conference and Celebration in Washington, D.C. in July, 1989. The initial draft, which included modifications from the Library Services to the Deaf Forum and Deaf Way meetings, was

---

[1] International Federation of Library Associations. Professional Board. Medium Term Programme 1986 - 1991. The Hague: IFLA Headquarters, 1988, pp 37 & 39.

reviewed by the Working Group and the Section during the 1989 IFLA General Conference in Paris and, after incorporating changes from that initial review, the draft was submitted to the World Federation for the Deaf for its examination. The proposed guidelines were subsequently reviewed by the World Federation for the Deaf during the meeting of its Management Committee in January 1990 in Vienna and by the Working Group and the Section Standing Committee in April. The modified draft was submitted for evaluation by the World Federation of the Deaf at its Board of Trustees meeting in Brighton in August 1990 where it was accepted for endorsement by the Federation. The final draft of the 1st edition then, with the endorsement of the World Federation of the Deaf was brought before the Section of Libraries Serving Disadvantaged Persons of the International Federation of Library Associations and Institutions where it received formal adoption at the 1990 General Conference in Stockholm.

The following documents were reviewed in the course of the development of these guidelines in order to ensure comprehensive coverage of the subject and to assist with the determination of consistent style and format. Particular credit must be given to Library Service to the Deaf and Hearing Impaired. Mrs. Dalton's work served as an overall benchmark in the preparation of these guidelines.

>American Library Association. Association of Specialized and Cooperative Library Agencies. "Techniques for Library Service to the Deaf and Hard of Hearing." INTERFACE. Fall, 1981.

>American Library Association. Committee on Standards. ALA Standards Manual. Chicago, Illinois: American Library Association, January 1983.

>Anderson, William. "Helping the Hard of Hearing". Unpublished manuscript, 1985.

>Association of Specialized and Cooperative Library Agencies. Ad Hoc Subcommittee on Standards for Multitype Library Cooperatives and Networks. "Multitype Draft Standards". INTERFACE. Vol. 11, (Fall 1988) 1, p. 4.

>Carroll, Frances Laverne, and Beilke, Patricia F. Guidelines for the Planning and Organization of School Library Centres, rev. ed., Paris: Unesco, 1979.

>Cylke, Frank Kurt, ed. Library Service for the Blind and Physically Handicapped: An International Approach. München, etc.: K.G. Saur (IFLA Publications 16), 1979.

>Dalton, Phyllis I. Library Service to the Deaf and Hearing Impaired. Phoenix, Arizona: The Oryx Press, 1985.

Hagemeyer, Alice. Tentative Guidelines for Library and Information Services to the Deaf Community. paper prepared for the American Library Association. (Photocopy.), 1988.

International Federation of Library Associations. Section of Libraries Serving Disadvantaged Persons. Guidelines for Libraries Serving Hospital Patients and Disabled People in the Community. The Hague: IFLA Headquarters, 1984 (IFLA Professional Reports, No. 2).

International Federation of Library Associations. Section of Public Libraries. Guidelines for Public Libraries. München, etc.: K.G. Saur (IFLA Publications 36), 1986.

International Federation of Library Associations. Section of Public Libraries. Standards for Public Libraries. Pullach/München: Verlag Dokumentation, 1973.

Lynch, Beverly, ed. "Standards for University Libraries". IFLA Journal, Vol. 13, (1987) 2, pp 120-25.

Massis, Bruce E., Ed. Library Service for the Blind and Physically Handicapped: An International Approach, Vol. 2. München, etc.: K.G. Saur (IFLA Publications 23), 1982.

Moon, Valerie. Opening Doors for Closed Ears: Proceedings of the Conference on Library Services for Deaf and Hearing Impaired People. Sydney: State Library of New South Wales, 1988.

New York Library Association. Roundtable for Libraries Serving Special Populations. Guidelines for Libraries Serving Persons with a Hearing Impairment or a Visual Impairment. New York: New York Library Association, July 1987.

Sorenson, Liene S. Taking Action to Enhance Public Library Services for Persons with Disabilities. Skokie, Illinois: Skokie Accessible Library Services, Skokie Public Library, 1988.

The following list of persons includes the 1990 members of the Standing Committee of the Section of Libraries Serving Disadvantaged Persons and others who gave freely of their time, effort, experience, and expertise in the development of the original guidelines.

W. Anderson	United Kingdom
J. Beaudin	United States of America
S. Bruhn	Australia
K-J. Carlsen	Norway
G. Chavanis	France
J. Coleman	United States of America

F. Czajkowski	Poland
P.I. Dalton	United States of America
A. Dobbie	New Zealand
A. Galler	Canada
T. Haimakainen	Finland
A. Hagemeyer	United States of America
F. Kaiser	The Netherlands
Y. Kikuchi	Japan
C. Law	Australia
G. Malmgren-Neale	Sweden
A. Melkis	Federal Republic of Germany
V. Moon	Australia
P. Noaks	United Kingdom
M. Peillon	France
B. Pors	Denmark
G. Rappaport-Bathenau	France
M. Starmans	The Netherlands
K. Thulin	Sweden
H. Wagenaar	The Netherlands

Particular recognition and credit must be given to the World Federation of the Deaf for its review, input, and endorsement of both the 1st and 2nd editions of these guidelines and it should be noted that both federations, IFLA and WFD, have established a formal joint Consultative Status relationship.

John Michael Day
University Librarian
Gallaudet University
Washington, DC
USA

Chair, Section of Libraries
Serving Disadvantaged Persons

2. INTRODUCTION

2.1 CONTEXT

For a number of reasons, most libraries have not considered focusing particular attention on the provision of services to persons who are deaf. Deafness has been called, with good reason, the "invisible handicap" because deaf people are not identifiable as deaf by casual observation and they tend to blend into the larger community. Additionally, people who are deaf from birth or from an early age often have difficulty reading and have a tendency to not use libraries. As a consequence, libraries and deaf people have mostly been unaware of each other; however, a substantial portion of the population is deaf and libraries have a responsibility to ensure that their collections and services are accessible to deaf people and that deaf people are aware of the services libraries can provide them.

The primary issue involved with the provision of services to deaf people is that communication often requires additional effort, knowledge, patience, and (where available) technological aids. The degree to which communicating with any individual deaf person requires these additional skills usually depends on the degree of hearing loss and the age at which the person experienced it, i.e., age of onset. Central to an understanding of these individual differences is an understanding of the difference that the age of onset can make. Generally, the older an individual is when the hearing loss is experienced, the more comfortable that individual is likely to be with indigenous oral and written languages. However, individuals who are born deaf or become deaf before acquiring speech may have speech that is difficult to understand or may use no speech at all, and may have difficulty with reading.

Because of this variation, and the variations in educational approaches, deaf people frequently have been arranged and rearranged into assorted categories under assorted labels. Librarians need to be aware of this variation and of the controversies regarding education and communication modes in order to build comprehensive and impartial collections of materials about deafness and of related materials otherwise of concern and interest to both deaf and hearing people. In designing library programs for deaf people, it is often useful to have one term to encompass all of the persons affected. Therefore, for that purpose, the term "deaf community" will be used in this document to refer to the following groups as a whole: native sign language users; users of native sign language and written language of the general public; oralists; late-deafened adults; hearing impaired elderly people; minimal language users; hard of hearing individuals; and hearing members of deaf persons' families. Professionals associated with services to the deaf community are also included. See "Deaf Community" under Section 4, "Definitions."

Libraries are often in the unique position of being a community's sole source of impartial information and, therefore, have a responsibility to collect and provide such information to their deaf clientele. It must be noted, however, that the primary goal of any specialized program to the Deaf Community must be to provide equal access to all programs and services that are enjoyed by the library's hearing clientele. The establishment of specialized programs and services is in response to the recognition of the additional needs of deaf clientele but the specialized program should not constitute the totality of the deaf clients' library experience.

2.2 PURPOSE AND SCOPE

These guidelines that follow are meant to inform librarians about the library and information needs of deaf people and pertain to all libraries that have deaf persons as any portion of their clientele. They apply to all types of libraries including public, school, and academic, as well as special libraries serving government, commerce and industry, the arts, military, hospitals, prisons and other institutions. They are statements of general principles and, as such, contain no quantitative prescriptions. They are, however, meant to serve both as an encouragement to establish services for deaf persons and as a means to assess the completeness and quality of such services. As these guidelines are international in scope, it must be understood that they need to be tempered by national and local limitations on practicality, e.g., the application of guidelines regarding the use of technology and technological aids should be dropped where such is not available.

Additionally, this document should serve as a guide in the development of national guidelines for library services to deaf people, as it may be easily modified to conform to local circumstances. In the absence of any local guidelines, these guidelines should apply.

3. GUIDELINES

3.1 PERSONNEL

3.1.1 Responsibility for the development, implementation, and operation of library services to the deaf community should be assigned to a professional librarian holding the degrees, certification, and/or training pertaining to such professional status.

COMMENTARY

Libraries strive to provide the best service possible to their clientele. It is imperative that the same level of service available to the general constituency of the library be equally available to clientele who are deaf. In order to achieve this goal, the attention of a trained, professional librarian is necessary in the design and operation of the service. The eventual continuing level of professional attention focused on the service will be dependent on many factors including the size of the library, the size of its general community, and the size of its deaf community. However, the amount of professional staff time devoted to the service should be sufficient according to the demands and practicalities of each library's individual circumstances. In libraries with a very small deaf community, the minimum might be that the design and supervision of the service would be done by a professional librarian having responsibility for a larger service in the district.

3.1.2 Library staff should receive training focusing on the issues involved in providing services to the deaf community.

COMMENTARY

In order to provide adequate and appropriate services to deaf people, it is necessary for staff persons to have an understanding of their special needs, including those relating to varying communication needs, deaf culture, special collections of materials, captioning of video programs, assistive listening devices, specialized alerting devices, technological communication aids, reading levels, etc. (see also 3.2.1 regarding staff training in communication techniques). In metropolitan areas, it may be possible to make arrangements with other local groups serving deaf people to provide staff awareness training on site. In other situations, it may only be possible to send one staff member to receive formal training and to have that person be responsible for providing training for the rest of the library staff.

3.1.3   When selecting staff to be involved with the provision of services to deaf people, libraries should attempt to employ persons who have or are likely to be able to obtain credibility within the deaf community.

COMMENTARY

As is the case with employing other minority groups, libraries have much to gain by hiring deaf staff members. Libraries may be able to hire one or more deaf professional librarians or non-professional staff members to have responsibilities for its services to the deaf community either full or part time. When selecting staff that will provide services to deaf people, libraries should, at a minimum, ensure that any person selected has the necessary training, background, and/or exhibits such personal characteristics as to lead one to expect that the person will be able to obtain credibility within the deaf community.

3.1.4   Schools of librarianship should provide training in the provision of services to the deaf community as a normal part of their basic curriculum to prepare librarians for their professional qualifications and as a part of their continuing education programs for all levels of library staff.

COMMENTARY

Many schools of librarianship currently offer training in how to serve diverse populations. Training in the provision of all types of services to deaf people should be a required part of the certification process for all professional librarians. This training might be a separate course wholly devoted to library services to the deaf community where the demand for such a course would justify its provision or it might logically be a part of a more general course on provision of services to all disadvantaged persons and/or people of diverse cultures.

3.1.5   Libraries having responsibilities at the national level, or where applicable at an appropriate regional level, should establish an office or department responsible for provision of advisory and consultation services to all libraries within their geographical boundaries in order to assist them in the provision of services to the deaf community.[2]

---

[2] International Federation of Library Associations. Section of Public Libraries. Guidelines for Public Libraries. München, etc.: K.G. Saur (IFLA Publications 36), 1986. See pp. 54-55, guideline #'s 6.9 and 6.10 under National Support Services.

COMMENTARY

Establishment of an office or department having responsibilities for the provision of such services within a geographical area has several advantages. First, it would function as a formal conduit for a network among all libraries providing services to deaf people and, thereby, ensure that the latest techniques, services, materials, etc. are communicated among those libraries; and, second, such an office would function as an incentive in the establishment of such service in all libraries within the geographical area. Depending on many factors, including the size of the geographical area covered, the number of libraries affected, and the size of the overall deaf population, this office might be responsible solely for services to deaf people, or it might have broader responsibilities, including services to additional groups of disadvantaged persons.

3.1.6 **Each national library association should establish a group within its structure that would function as that portion of its membership focusing on the provision of library services to the deaf community.**

COMMENTARY

Librarians who are concerned with the provision of services to deaf people have much to gain by assembling to discuss issues of common interest, to make recommendations to the national association for action, and to share information. Additionally, such an assembly would be able to effectively function as an advocate of library services to the deaf community.

3.2 COMMUNICATION

3.2.1 **All library staff should receive training in how to communicate effectively with deaf people.**

COMMENTARY

People who are deaf communicate with hearing people in a variety of ways. Depending on their background, degree of hearing disability, cultural identity, and the situation, deaf people may use sign language, speak, write, gesture, or use any combination of the above. In the provision of library services, it is essential that library staff be aware of this variety and that they have the training necessary to know what to do in order to understand and to make themselves understood comfortably. Libraries with a large deaf clientele should seriously consider ensuring that at least one staff member who has responsibilities for the provision of services to deaf people be at least moderately fluent in sign language and that other public service personnel have experience with basic signing as appropriate.

3.2.2 **A text telephone (TTY) should be available at each main service point, e.g., the reference desk, in each library. Additionally, at least one TTY should be available for use by library clientele to make telephone calls from the library if the making of such calls is available to hearing clientele.[3]**

COMMENTARY

TTY's are the means by which deaf people make use of the telephone. Where hearing people can call into the library for reference services or to find information regarding library hours and other general information, and where libraries provide telephones for use by their clientele in making outgoing calls, those libraries should provide the means, i.e., TTY's, for deaf people to access those same services. All members of the library staff should receive training in the use of the TTY.

3.2.3 **Telephones for use by library clientele or staff should be equipped with amplification.**

COMMENTARY

Amplifiers, i.e., volume control devices, assist persons with sufficient residual hearing to use the telephone without the use of a TTY. Libraries that provide telephones for use by their staff and clientele should provide handset amplifiers or other such assistive devices for persons who depend on them to use telephones effectively.

3.2.4 **Libraries should ensure that their Internet presence is wholly accessible.**

COMMENTARY

Where libraries maintain an electronic presence on the Internet or World Wide Web, they need to make sure that all of the information presented is accessible to their deaf clientele. All audio tracks should be open-captioned and audio

---

[3] Recent advances in technology have made available new assistive devices that fall within this section on communication, e.g., TTY's (3.2.2), audio loops (3.2.6), etc. It is understood that these devices will not be readily available in many parts of the world and should be disregarded where such is the case. Nonetheless, the spirit of the guidelines in this section indicates that libraries should make use of whatever appropriate technological aids are available to them in the provision of services to their deaf population.

files should also be available as downloadable transcript files. Wherever audio feedback is given for interactions, e.g., a "click" sound when a web page button is selected, visual feedback should also be given, e.g., the button flashes on the screen.

3.2.5 **Libraries should use the latest advantages in technology for communicating with deaf people where such technology has proven beneficial within the deaf community.**

COMMENTARY

In addition to using TTY's for real-time communication with their deaf clientele, libraries should use whatever technology, largely accepted by the deaf community, in order to ensure easy and comfortable communication. For example, electronic mail (email) has proven to be a highly effective mode of communication among deaf people and between deaf and hearing people; and, wherever Internet services are available, email access to the library should be made available. As technology changes, libraries should be aware of communication modes accepted and widely used by their deaf clientele since, over time, email may be surpassed by newer, more effective means of communication.

3.2.6 **Libraries should have communication aids such as assistive listening systems and equipment that can be used to support computer-assisted real-time captioning or computer-assisted note taking. These services should be available for meetings and programs upon request.**

COMMENTARY

Assistive listening systems, e.g., FM systems, infrared systems, audio loops, etc., are used by persons with hearing disabilities who need them to enhance auditory information. By using these assistive devices, many patrons can better understand lectures, meetings, music, and other programs. Computer-assisted real-time captioning and computer-assisted note taking allow patrons who do not benefit from interpreters or assistive listening devices to see a running text of information as it is being shared. Communications technology is changing rapidly, and libraries should maintain awareness of current developments.

3.2.7 **Libraries with television viewing facilities should provide closed caption television decoders for use by their clientele.**

COMMENTARY

Depending on the local captioning standard, libraries should be collecting videotapes for client use which are closed captioned, open captioned, or signed (see section 3.3.4). Where libraries are collecting closed-captioned videotapes, they should provide closed caption decoders so that the videotapes may be used by those persons depending on captioning for their understanding. Where libraries provide closed captioned videotapes for home use, they should also provide for loan of closed captioned decoders so that access to the same level of information and service is available to all deaf people regardless of their ability to purchase the technology for themselves.

3.2.8 **Libraries should offer to provide sign language and oral interpreters, computer-assisted real-time captioning, or computer-assisted note taking services for all library-sponsored programs upon request.**

COMMENTARY

Library-related programs that are open to the public, e.g., bibliographic instruction, computer orientation, research workshops, storytelling, etc., must be accessible to clientele who have a variety of communication needs. Sign language and/or oral interpreter services and/or electronic text services should be provided at the library's expense when any library user who depends on one of these accommodations has made a commitment to attend.

3.2.9 **Libraries should install visible warning signals in order to alert deaf clientele to problems and emergencies.**

COMMENTARY

Since deaf people cannot hear auditory signals such as fire alarms, public address and security alarming devices, it is essential that libraries install visible systems for alerting their deaf clientele to announcements and to emergency situations. Such systems should include the addition of flashing lights, or other appropriate visual signals, wherever an auditory signal is produced. An inspection of the library premises or an evacuation exercise should ensure that all library staff and clientele have received any announcement and/or notification of an emergency situation.

3.3 COLLECTIONS

3.3.1 **Libraries should collect materials related to deafness and Deaf culture that will be of interest to both deaf and hearing clientele.**

COMMENTARY

The primary objective of any program to provide services to deaf people will be to incorporate deaf people into the library's general clientele in making use of all of the library's collections, programs, and services. However, libraries should also collect materials of special interest to deaf people and to hearing people who will need information or will have a general interest in deafness. Such materials would include current and historical materials related to deafness, works by and about deaf artists and other famous deaf people, materials related to sign languages and other communication modes, government documents, legal materials and periodicals related to deafness, etc. Because the full range of resources should be open to the library's deaf clientele, these materials should not be maintained as a physically separate collection but should be integrated into the total resources of the library.

3.3.2 **Libraries should collect, maintain, and offer information about educational options, referral agencies, and programs for deaf people in a wholly unbiased fashion.**

COMMENTARY

Methods employed in the education of deaf people and their modes of communication have constituted areas of intense controversy and competition for many years. Libraries are often in a unique position of providing complete information from an impartial and dispassionate perspective. Because of this position, libraries have the responsibility to exercise caution in ensuring that they collect materials from all viewpoints, particularly in such areas as information for deaf people, their parents, their other family members, and practitioners about programs and referral agencies.

3.3.3 **Libraries should assemble and provide access to a collection of high interest / low reading level materials of interest to deaf people.**[4]

COMMENTARY

For many deaf people, mastery of the oral and written idiom is a particular challenge. Libraries should strive to acquire general materials that may be

---

[4] In some countries, these are known as "Easy-to-Read Materials" or "Easy Readers."

understood by as many of their clientele as possible. Additionally, libraries should build and actively maintain a collection of high interest materials which are written purposefully with direct and simple vocabulary and which are heavily illustrated where appropriate so that they may be easily understood by people who have yet to gain full mastery of the local oral and written language, including many deaf people as well as people from other linguistic minorities.

3.3.4 **Visual non-print materials should form an integral part of any library's collections acquired in support of services to deaf clientele. Television video programs and other such media with audio portions should be captioned or signed so that they may be understood by persons unable to hear.**

COMMENTARY

Because deaf people need to rely on sight, visual media offer a particularly effective means of communicating information. Also, where one of the library's goals is to offer materials of an entertainment nature, television videotapes are especially attractive. Collecting videotapes produced with an open caption format would be the most efficient; however, where such is not desirable, libraries should collect closed-captioned videotapes and provide decoding equipment as necessary. See paragraph 3.2.7.

3.3.5 **Libraries should assemble and maintain a collection of videotapes and/or films in sign language and provide sufficient equipment necessary to view them.**

COMMENTARY

Sign language is the basic communication means in the lives of many deaf people. Some countries produce video programs or films in sign language; e.g., translations of television programs, fairy tales, deaf folklore, news programs, sign language instruction, etc. Where available, libraries should collect and lend such media as an essential service to deaf people, parents with deaf children, and people learning sign language.

3.4 SERVICES

3.4.1 **All of the library's collections, services, and programs should be made accessible to its deaf community.**

COMMENTARY

In addition to whatever specialized services libraries establish as part of their programs in support of their deaf community, it is imperative that libraries design and implement such programs with the fundamental understanding that these programs are only a part of and are in addition to the primary objective of making all of the libraries' collections, services, and programs which are accessible to hearing people also accessible to deaf people. For instance, where libraries provide training in the use of access technology, e.g., training in the use of the World Wide Web for searching, sign language interpretation of the training should be offered and publicized.

3.4.2 **Members of the library's deaf community, as defined in these guidelines, should be involved in the design and development of the library's services to deaf people, including the development of services and collections, and in the establishment of advisory committees, service organizations, and networks.**

COMMENTARY

The success of any service depends upon its content and quality and upon the acceptance of the service by the clientele for whom it is designed. Until such time as a program of services has been established and is proven popular and successful within the library's deaf clientele, it may be necessary for the individual who is responsible for program design to go out into the community and to actively solicit interest and assistance from deaf individuals. After such relationships are established, the continued success of the service will depend on the continued success of this network between the library and the deaf community.

3.4.3 **Libraries should offer programs conducted in sign language.**

COMMENTARY

Libraries become, by nature, major cultural centers in their communities and often provide both cultural and social programs. It is essential that all programs and public meetings held in libraries be made accessible by provision of sign language interpreters, oral interpreters, computer-assisted real-time captioning, or computer assisted note taking as requested. Nevertheless, some programs should be offered for deaf clientele in sign language, with voice interpreters for hearing clientele. Provision of programs in sign language, e.g., storytelling and programs related to Deaf culture, would be of interest and benefit to all groups within the community.[5]

3.4.4 **Libraries should provide information on local literacy programs that are accessible to deaf non-readers. Libraries should ensure that library-sponsored literacy programs meet the needs of deaf individuals.**

COMMENTARY

Many persons who were either born deaf or deafened at an early age have difficulty learning to read because they did not grow up hearing the local spoken language. Each country's sign language, the language of many of its deaf people, has a grammatical structure entirely different from that of the local spoken language. Libraries must consider the unique needs of deaf individuals when developing literacy programs, at a minimum by consulting with professionals knowledgeable about methods used to educate deaf students.

3.4.5 **Libraries should include local deaf-related information in its online community information and referral database.**

COMMENTARY

With the emergence of the World Wide Web (WWW), many libraries have created online community information and referral databases in order to provide a central reference point for local community information. Because electronic communication and the WWW have proven to be extraordinarily effective media for deaf people, it is important that libraries use such means to provide local information of particular interest to their deaf clientele.

3.4.6 **Libraries should include an unbiased variety of deaf-related electronic links in their online databases.**

COMMENTARY

Deaf and deaf-related organizations worldwide have made exceptional use of the World Wide Web in providing information of interest to deaf people. Particularly because of the unusual extent and richness of reference, cultural, and news information provided online by and for deaf people, it is a responsibility of libraries to provide access to such information where such

---

[5] International Federation of Library Associations. Section of Public Libraries. Guidelines for Public Libraries. München, etc.: K.G. Saur (IFLA Publications 36), 1986, p. 19, "Cultural and Social Provisions" and p. 24, Guidelines # 1.81.

libraries have access to the World Wide Web. Wherever possible, libraries providing such links should enlist the assistance of a broad spectrum of their deaf community in ensuring that their collected links encompass the wide variety of philosophical and cultural viewpoints regarding deaf people and Deaf culture (see Guideline 3.3.2 and attendant commentary).

3.5 PROGRAM MARKETING

3.5.1 Libraries should aggressively market their programs and services to their deaf community.

COMMENTARY

Because people who are deaf from birth or an early age very often have difficulty with reading, they have a tendency, in general, to not use libraries. It is essential, therefore, for libraries to target their deaf clientele for special marketing efforts; otherwise, labor and resources allocated for providing services will have minimal value. For these same reasons, this effort will need particularly careful planning.

3.5.2 All library publicity should provide for access to the library's deaf community.

COMMENTARY

Libraries need to make use of all available means to inform their communities of their accessibility to deaf people. They should include the TTY number on all stationery, announcements, brochures, fliers, etc. and ensure that all televised information and promotions are captioned. All general library publications should include information on programs and services for deaf people.

4. DEFINITIONS

The following terms are used in this document and the definitions given are meant only to assist in understanding and applying these guidelines in libraries. No application of these terms outside of the limits of this document is intended.

Assistive Listening System   A hearing enhancement system consisting of a transmitter and a receiver - generally a hearing aid or a device connected to a hearing aid - designed to eliminate the background noise interference caused by extraneous factors. There are several different types of communication access systems, e.g., audio loop systems, AM systems, FM sound systems, and infrared systems.

Audio Loop   See **Assistive Listening System**

Captioned   Refers to films, or video programs, where the dialogue is also shown, in print, on the screen along with the rest of the picture. The printed dialogue may be either always visible (open captioned) or visible only with the addition of a decoder machine (closed captioned) that translates the invisible signal into visible print.

Closed Captioned   See **Captioned**

Computer-Assisted Note Taking   A system whereby a note taker types on a computer keyboard what is being said during a meeting. After a short lag time, the notes are displayed on a projection screen or a monitor.

Computer-Assisted Real-Time Captioning   A system whereby a highly skilled court reporter uses a shorthand machine and a computer to translate spoken language into written text. The verbatim text may be read on a video monitor or on a projection screen immediately.

Deaf Community	This term has different meanings in different contexts. For the purposes of this document, it refers to: • Sign language users • Bilingual users of sign language and spoken or written language • Persons with hearing disabilities who communicate primarily through spoken language and speech reading • Late-deafened adults • Older adults with hearing loss due to age • Deaf people who use neither sign language nor written language • Hard of hearing individuals • Deaf-blind individuals • Hearing family members • Professionals who serve the above
Deaf Person	A person who is either partially or wholly unable to hear.
Decoder	A machine which, when attached to or built into a television, translates the electronic signals of a closed captioned video program into words printed on the screen along with the rest of the video images.
Easy-to-Read Materials	High interest / low reading level materials, including captioned media, for all groups with reading or comprehension problems regardless of age.
Hard-of-Hearing Individual	A person who has a mild to moderate hearing loss.
Interpreters	Individuals skilled at translating spoken communication into either sign language or clear oral speech. **Sign Language Interpreters** are skilled at translating the meaning of spoken language into sign language and translating sign language into

spoken words. **Oral Interpreters** silently mouth a speaker's words for a deaf person who communicates primarily by using spoken language and speechreading. They use no sign language and are skilled at making substitutions for words that are difficult to speechread.

Late-Deafened Adult	An adult who loses hearing after acquiring speech and experiences a significant life change as a result.
Minimal Language User	A person who has very limited knowledge of any formal spoken, signed, or written language.
Native Sign Language User	A person whose first language is sign language.
Open Captioned	See **Captioned**
Oralist	A person who is deaf and who communicates primarily through speech and speech reading.
TDD	See **TTY**
TTY	A device with an electronic text display and a keyboard that allows persons with hearing or speech disabilities to have a visual, two-way telephone conversation.
Visual Warning Signal	A flashing or revolving light that draws the attention of deaf people to audible signals such as fire alarms or public announcements.

あとがき

　IFLA指針第2版では「1.はじめに」で述べられているように、新たにインターネット等のコンピュータ関連の指摘が多くなされました。
　この分野については、日本でも「日本聴覚障害者コンピュータ協会」が編集した『聴覚障害者とインターネット』（中央法規出版　1999年刊）が出版されております。この本は、聴覚障害者向けに聴覚障害者の視点で書かれたものですが、図書館にとっても重要な指摘がいくつも書かれています。
　第1章には「電子メールは文章だけでやりとりしますから、電話のように耳を使わなくてすむ」とあります。電話を使うのが難しい聴覚障害者にとって、ファクシミリは通信手段の主流ですが、ファクシミリを持ち歩くことはできません。その点、携帯電話やPHSの電子メールは、外出先でも送受信することができます。例えば図書館に予約した本の貸出準備ができたというような連絡を、外出中でも受け取ることができます。
　しかし、欠点もいくつかあります。この本には「文章を上手に書くことのできない聴覚障害者が多いということも問題の一つになっている」(p.55)と書かれています。
　聴覚障害者は耳から言葉が入ってきません。そのため、特に言語獲得前に失聴した聴覚障害者の中には、文章自体を書くことが苦手な人がたくさんいます。たとえ漢字を知っていても、正しい読みを覚えることが難しいために、読みを入力して漢字変換するのがうまくいかない人もいます。
　手書き文字入力という方法もありますが、ファクシミリのほうが楽に

書くことができます。

　文章を書くことが苦手な人には指針3.4.4のように識字プログラムが必要であるし、入力はできないが文字は書ける人にはファクシミリも必要です。

　また、聴覚障害者がインターネットを利用しない理由として「電子メールの教育を十分に受けていないもしくは受けられない聴覚障害者がたくさんいる」(p.55) ことや「講座の多くは手話通訳者など聴覚障害者のための情報保障が用意されていない」(同) ことが書かれています。指針でも3.4.3に手話通訳やパソコン要約筆記を付ける必要性が書かれています。

　日本語の読み書きが苦手な聴覚障害者にとって、利用教育なしでマニュアルや説明書だけでインターネットや電子メールを使うことは困難です。そのためにも手話通訳や要約筆記などの情報保障に努めてください。

　指針の「4. 定義」で新たに出てきた「パソコン要約筆記」(最近は「パソコン文字通訳」とも言われています) は日本でも徐々に広まりつつあります。パソコン要約筆記のためのソフトも無料で配布されていますし、数は少ないのですが勉強会も開かれています。キーボードからの入力は慣れた人なら手で書くより早く入力できるうえ、よく使われる単語は前もって登録しておけるので、話されていることを手書きの要約筆記よりも多く早く入力することができます。

　『聴覚障害者とインターネット』では、インターネットを利用したテレビ電話についても紹介されています。この本ではCU-SeeMeというソフトが取り上げられていますが、現在ではMSN Messenger と Net Meeting を使う方法やYahoo! Messengerなどが普及しつつあります。どちらのソフトにもビデオチャット (テレビ電話) 機能があり、無料で配布されています。

　聴覚障害者にとって、文字だけでなく顔や表情が見える方がずっとコ

ミュニケーションをとりやすくなります。インターネットの通信スピードやカメラの性能向上などにより、ビデオチャットによる手話での会話が広まるのも遠い話ではないのかもしれません。

　聴覚障害者に受け入れられているさまざまな手段を図書館が用意することにより、聴覚障害者は図書館に問い合わせや、予約、レファレンスの依頼、行事への参加がしやすくなります。ウェブサイトを持っていたり、Web-OPACを公開している図書館に対しては、開館日や所蔵の有無といった程度の内容でしたら、ウェブサイトにアクセスすれば、メールで問い合わせるよりすぐに知りたいことがわかります。ウェブサイトを持っている図書館、またはこれから作ろうとしている図書館は、聴覚障害者も利用しているということも考え、指針3.2.4のように音声だけの情報は、見てわかるよう文字情報などを入れて下さい。

　技術の進歩は非常に早いものがあります。ここで紹介したことも、すぐに古い技術となるでしょう。常に新しい技術に目を向け、取り入れてください。

　なおこの指針では、日本で一般的に使われている「ホームページ」という語は使わず、「ウェブサイト」と表しました。そのため、多少わかりにくい表現になったかもしれません。これは、コンピュータ用語は変わりやすいこと、ホームページのもとの意味はトップページのみを指す言葉であること、指針なので訳語の正確性が求められること等から、あえてこの表現をとらせていただきました。

　私たちのグループは、聴覚障害者に対する図書館サービスのあり方を考えることを目的に、1984年、日本図書館協会障害者サービス委員会の中に「聴覚障害者に対する図書館サービスを考えるワーキンググループ」として設立されました。2002年には日本図書館協会の委員会再編に伴い、「聴覚障害者に対する図書館サービスを考えるグループ」と名

称を変更しました。

　『聴覚障害者も使える図書館に－図書館員のためのマニュアル－』の初版を1986年に出版したほか、日本図書館協会障害者サービス委員会編の『すべての人に図書館サービスを－障害者サービス入門－』、『障害者サービス』(図書館員選書　12)の聴覚障害者関係部分を執筆する等、聴覚障害者に対する図書館サービスの必要性を訴えてきました。

　1998年には『聴覚障害者も使える図書館に－図書館員のためのマニュアル－』の改訂版を出版しましたので、今回の指針第2版と合わせてお読みいただければ幸いです。

　翻訳には、斎藤禎子、松延秀一、渡辺修の3名があたり、編集は日本図書館協会事務局の協力を得て、椎原綾子が担当いたしました。

　この指針第2版の出版が、日本の図書館における聴覚障害者サービスの開始・拡大につながるならば、当グループにとってそれ以上の喜びはありません。

　　　　　日本図書館協会障害者サービス委員会
　　　　　　　聴覚障害者に対する図書館サービスを考えるグループ

訳者一覧

斎藤　禎子（聴覚障害者に対する図書館サービスを考えるグループ）
松延　秀一（京都大学総合人間学部図書館・聴覚障害者に対する図書館サービスを考えるグループ）
渡辺　修　（聴覚障害者に対する図書館サービスを考えるグループ）

聴覚障害者に対する図書館サービスのためのIFLA指針　第2版

1993年10月30日　初版発行
2003年 3月31日　第2版発行

定　価　　本体1000円（税別）

編　者　　ジョン・マイケル・デイ
訳　者　　日本図書館協会障害者サービス委員会
　　　　　聴覚障害者に対する図書館サービスを考えるグループ
発行者　　社団法人　日本図書館協会
　　　　　〒104-0033　東京都中央区新川1-11-14
　　　　　Tel 03-3523-0811㈹　Fax 03-3523-0817
印刷所　　㈱ワープ

JLA200242　　　　　　　　　　　　　　　　　　　Printed in Japan

ISBN4-8204-0229-3

本文の用紙は中性紙を使用しています。